像无人观望一样跳舞

浩瀚◎编

厦门大学出版社
XIAMEN UNIVERSITY PRESS
国家一级出版社
全国百佳图书出版单位

目　录

Things That School Doesn't Teach You

Bill Gates used these ten rules for a high school speech. His honesty is commendable①.

Rule 1 Life is not fair—get used to it.

Rule 2 The world won't care about your self-esteem②. The world will expect you to accomplish something before you feel good about yourself.

Rule 3 You will not make 50 thousand dollars a year right out of high school. You won't be a vice president with a luxury vehide, until you earn both.

Rule 4 If you think your teacher is tough, wait till you get a boss. He doesn't have tenure③.

Rule 5 Flipping burgers is not beneath your dignity. Your grandparents had a different word for burger flipping; they called it opportunity.

Rule 6 If you mess up, it's not your parents' fault, so don't whine about your mistakes, learn from them.

Rule 7 Before you were born, your parents weren't as boring as they are now. They got that way from paying your bills, cleaning your clothes and listening your talking talk about how cool you are. So before you save the rainforest from the parasites④ of your parents' generation, try delousing⑤ the closet in your own room.

Rule 8 Your school may have done away with winners and losers, but life has not. In some schools they have abolished failing grades and they'll give you as many times as you want to get the right answer. This doesn't bear the slightest resemblance⑥ to anything in real life.

Rule 9 Life is not divided into semesters⑦. You don't get summers off and very few employers are interested in helping you find yourself. Do that on your own time.

Rule 10 Television is not real life. In real life people actually have to leave the coffee shop and go to jobs.

词汇

① commendable 值得赞美的,很好的

② self-esteem 自尊

③ tenure 任期

④ parasite 寄生虫,食客

⑤ delouse 除去……的虱子

⑥ resemblance 相似,形似

⑦ semester 学期

学校没教给你的道理

比尔·盖茨在一所中学演讲中提到了这10条规则，他的坦率着实可嘉。

第一条　人生是不公平的，习惯接受吧。

第二条　这个世界并不在乎你的自尊，它会先希冀你有所成就，然后才是你是否自我感觉良好。

第三条　你不会一离开高中就有五万美元年薪，你不会马上成为拥有豪华房车的副总裁，你必须靠努力赚取。

第四条　如果你觉得老师很凶，等你有了老板你就知道了。老板不像老师，他没有任期。

第五条　在快餐店打工煎汉堡并不可耻。你的祖父母对煎汉堡有不同的看法：那是机会。

第六条　如果你一事无成，不是你父母的错，所以不要对自己犯的错发牢骚，从错误中去学习。

第七条　在你出生前，你的父母并不像现在这般无趣，他们变成这样是因为忙着付你的开销、洗你的衣服、听你吹嘘你有多了不起。所以在拯救被父母这代人所豢养的寄生虫破坏的热带雨林前，请你先整理好自己的房间。

第八条　在学校里可能有赢家输家，在人生中却还言之过早。学校会不断给你机会找到正确答案，真实人生却完全不是这么回事。

第九条　人生没有寒暑假，人生不是学期制，没有哪个雇主有兴趣帮你寻找自我，请用自己的时间来寻找自我吧。

第十条　电视上演的并非真实人生，现实生活中人们不得不离开咖啡馆去工作。

Fisherman

There was a group called "The Fisherman's Fellowship". They were surrounded by streams and lakes full of hungry fish. They met regularly[①] to discuss the call to fish, and the thrill of catching fish. They got excited about fishing.

Someone suggested that they needed a philosophy of fishing, so they carefully defined and redefined fishing, and the purpose of fishing. They developed fishing strategies and tactics[②]. Then they realized that they had been going at it backwards. They had approached fishing from the point of view of the fisherman, and not from the point of view of the fish. How do fish view the world? How does the fisherman appear to the fish? What do fish eat, and when? These are all good things to know. So they began research studies, and attended conferences on fishing. Some traveled to far-away places to study different kinds of fish, with different habits. Some got PhD's in fishology. But no one had yet gone fishing.

So a committee③ was formed to send out fishermen. As prospective fishing places outnumbered fishermen, the committee needed to determine priorities④.

A priority list of fishing places was posted on bulletin boards in all of the fellowship halls. But still, no one was fishing. A survey was launched, to find out why ... Most did not answer the survey, but from those that did, it was discovered that some felt called to study fish, a few to furnish fishing equipment, and several to go around encouraging the fisherman.

With meetings, conferences, and seminars, they just simply didn't have time to fish.

The members of the Fisherman's Fellowship were many, and the fish were plentiful, but the fishers were few.

词汇

① regularly 有规律地;经常地

② tactic 手段;策略;战术

③ committee 委员会

④ priority 优先(权);优先的事物

垂钓者

在一个河湖密布、鱼虾成群的地方有一个“钓鱼者协会”，协会的每个成员都是钓鱼的热衷者。他们时常聚在一起畅谈钓鱼的心得和钓鱼所带来的种种欢乐。

其中有人提出，应该对钓鱼形成一套理论。因此，他们谨慎地对钓鱼和钓鱼的目的进行了反复的定义，甚至还得出了关于钓鱼的战略和战术。但很快他们又意识到这样去研究钓鱼其实是一个倒退，因为他们仍然是从渔夫的角度而不是从鱼本身的角度来探讨钓鱼这一行为。在鱼的眼里，世界究竟是怎么样的？渔夫的出现对鱼又意味着什么？鱼吃什么，何时进食？这些才是需要弄懂的问题。于是他们又开始了新的调查研究，参加各种各样的关于钓鱼的讨论会，有些人还不辞千里到各地研究不同种类、不同习性的鱼，有些甚至还成了

研究鱼类的理论博士，但是他们当中没有一个真正去钓过鱼。

考虑到可供钓鱼的地方多而钓鱼者少，协会为此还专门成立了一个委员会来评估各种钓鱼场所，并给这些场所排名。

于是，协会各个大厅的公告栏上都贴了一份名册表注明哪些地方可以优先钓鱼，但结果还是没有人去钓。为什么会出现这种现象呢？协会又发起了问卷调查，大部分人没有反应，但从那些填写了问卷的人那里可以得知，有些人是在忙着研究鱼类，有些是在忙着完善钓鱼的装备，还有一些正在忙着到处发动人们去钓鱼。

太多的聚会，太多的研讨会要开，使得他们根本就没有时间去钓鱼。

钓鱼者协会的会员很多，水里的鱼也很多，但真正的钓鱼者却没有几个。

More Beautiful Than Freckles ①

An elderly man and her little granddaughter, whose face was sprinkled with bright freckles, spent the day at the zoo. Lots of children were waiting in line to get their cheeks painted by a local artist who was decorating them with tiger paws.

"You've got so many freckles, there's no place to paint!" a boy in the line said to the little girl.

Embarrassed, the little girl dropped her head. Her grandpa knelt down next to her. "I love your freckles. When I was a little boy I always wanted freckles," he said, tracing his fingers across the child's cheek. "Freckles are beautiful."

The girl looked up, "Really?"

"Of course," said the grandfather. "Why just name me one thing that's prettier than freckles?"

The little girl thought for a moment, peered intensely into

his grandpa's face, and softly whispered, "Wrinkles[2]."

词汇

① freckle 雀斑,斑点

② wrinkle 皱纹

比雀斑还美

一位老爷爷和他长满雀斑的小孙女一起在动物园里游玩。很多小孩都在排队等候一位当地的艺术家用虎爪在他们的脸上着色。

“你脸上这么多雀斑，都没地方画了！”队列中有个男孩子对小女孩说。

小女孩感到很难堪，低下了头。爷爷蹲下来对她说：“我喜欢你的雀斑，我小时候总想长这些雀斑呢。”他抚摸着女孩的脸颊，“雀斑很漂亮！”

女孩抬起头，“真的吗？”

“当然是真的，”爷爷说，“你看我身上有什么比雀斑还漂亮的？”

小女孩想了一下，又认真地注视着爷爷的面孔，小声地说：“皱纹。”

Dance Like No One Is Watching

We always convince ourselves that life will be better after we get married, have a baby, then another. Then we are frustrated that the kids aren't old enough and we'll be more content[①] when they are. After that we're frustrated that we have teenagers to deal with. We will certainly be happy when they are out of that stage.

We always tell ourselves that our life will be complete when our spouse[②] gets his or her act together, when we get a nicer car, and are able to go on a nice vacation, when we retire. The truth is, there's no better time than right now. If not now, when? Our life will always be filled with challenges. It's best to admit this to ourselves and decide to be happy anyway.

One of my favorite quotes[③] comes from Alfred Souza. He said, "For a long time it had seemed to me that life was about to begin—real life. But there was always some obstacle[④] in the way, so mething to be gotten through first, some unfinished business, time still to be served, a debt to be paid. Then life would begin. At last it dawned onto me that these obstacles were my life." This perspective has helped me to see that there is no way to happiness. Happiness is the way. So treasure every moment that you have. And remember that time waits for no one. So stop waiting until you finish school, until you go back to school; until you get married, until you get divorced; until you have kids, until your kids leave home; until you start work, until you retire; until you get a new car or home; until spring; until you are born again to decide that there is no better time than right now to be happy …

Happiness is a journey, not a destination. Therefore,
Work like you don't need money,
Love like you've never been hurt,
And dance like no one's watching.

① content 知足;满足;满意;愉快

② spouse 配偶

③ quote 引用,援引;引文

④ obstacle 障碍;妨害物

像无人观望一样跳舞

我们总是相信，等我们结了婚生了孩子，生活才会更美好。等有了孩子，我们又因为他们不够大而烦恼，想着等他们大些时，我们就会开心了。可等他们进入青少年时期，我们还是同样地苦恼，于是又相信等他们过了这一阶段，幸福就会到来。

我们总是告诉自己，等夫妻间任一方肯合作，等我们拥有更好的车，等我们能去度一次美妙的假期，等我们退休后，我们的生活一定会完美的。而事实的真相是，没有任何时刻比现在更宝贵。倘若不是现在，又会是何时？我们的生活每时每刻都会有挑战。最好是让自己接受这一事实，无论如何也要使自己保持快乐的心境。

我很欣赏艾尔弗雷德·苏泽的一段名言。他说：“长期以来，我都觉得生活——真正的生活似乎即将开始。可是总会遇到某种障碍，比如得先完成一些事情，没做完的工作、要花费的时间、该付的债务等等，之后生活才会开始。最后我醒悟过来了，这些障碍本身就是我的生活。”这一观点让我意识到，没有什么通往幸福的道路。幸福本身就是路。所以，珍惜你拥有的每一刻。记住，时不我待，不要再作所谓的等待——等你上完学，等你再回到学校；等你结婚或离婚；等你有了孩子或孩子长大离开家；等你开始工作或等你退休；等你有了新车或新房；等春天来临；等你有幸再来世上走一遭才明白此时此刻最应快乐……

幸福是一个旅程，而不是终点。所以，

尽情工作吧，就像你无需金钱；

尽情去爱吧，就像你从未被伤害过；

纵情起舞吧，就像根本无人观望。

Do What You Love Most

Three years ago, Susan of Indiana found herself getting up earlier and earlier, and going to bed later and later, just to meet everyday demands. The wife, mother and ophthalmic technician met her responsibilities, but lacked time for the things that mattered most.

She and her husband, Sully, an attorney[1], began searching for ways to simplify their lives. "We had to decide what was really important", says Susan. They knew they wanted more time to play with their four-year-old son, Abbey, to exercise and eat right, and to nurture[2].

So the couple chose to live more modestly, shopping with care for necessities and enjoying inexpensive pleasures such as reading, cooking and going to the park. Susan quit her job and began working part time from home. She printed up business cards that read "At your service—buy yourself a little time", and hired herself out for personal tasks such as shopping, paying bills, organizing parties, doing Internet Research—whatever clients[③] needed.

"I still work hard, but being able to control my hours makes all the difference," she says. "I can carve out time to take my son to the zoo or play basketball with him. My stress headaches are gone. Having a chance to get to know neighbors not only has been fun, but also helped us further simplify[④]."

词汇

① attorney　律师

② nurture　养育;教养;教育

③ client　顾客,主顾

④ simplify　使(某事物)简单或简明;简化

做你想做的事

三年前，印第安那州的苏珊发现，为了满足日常的生活需求，自己起床的时间越来越早，上床睡觉的时间也越来越晚。她履行着做妻子、母亲、眼科技师的责任，可是总是没有时间做她认为最重要的事情。

她的丈夫沙列是一名律师。他们开始寻找各种简化生活的方法。“我们需要确定什么才是真正重要的。”苏珊说。他们明白，多一些时间与四岁的儿子阿比一起玩耍、做运动，让他吃好，培养他们之间的感情，是他们共同的心愿。

于是，他们选择更适度地节俭生活，只买必需的用品，享受诸如阅读、烹饪、去公园等低消费的娱乐。苏珊辞掉了工作，开始做兼职。她印制了这样的名片：为您服务——节省您的时间。她受雇做一些私人的工作，如为他人购物、付款、组织聚会、作因特网调查等——只要顾客需要。

“尽管我工作还是辛苦，可是我能够控制自己的时间，这使一切都变得不同。”她说，“我能抽出时间带儿子去动物园，或者和他一起打篮球。压力引发的头痛也好了，也有了了解邻居的机会。这不仅带给我喜悦，也使我们的生活进一步简单化。”

Interview[①] God

"Come in," God said to me, "so, you would like to interview[①] me?"

"If you have the time," I said.

He smiled through his beard and said, "My time is called eternity and is enough to do everything. What questions do you have in mind to ask me?"

"None that are new to you. What's the one thing that surprises you most about mankind[②]?"

He answered, "That they get bored of being children, are in a rush to grow up, and then long to be children again. That they lose their health to make money and then lose their money to restore their health. That by thinking anxiously about the future, they forget the present, such that they live neither for the present nor the future. That they live as if they will never die, and they die as if they never had never lived ...”

His hands took mine and we were silent. After a long period, I said, “May I ask you another question?”

He replied with a smile.

“As a Father, what would you ask your children to do for the new year?”

“To learn that they cannot make anyone love them. What they can do is to let themselves be loved.

To learn that it takes years to build trust, and a few seconds to destroy it.

To learn that what is most valuable is not what they have in their lives, but who they have in their lives.

To learn that it is not good to compare themselves to others. There will be others better or worse than they are.

To learn that a rich person is not one who has the most, but is one who needs the least.”

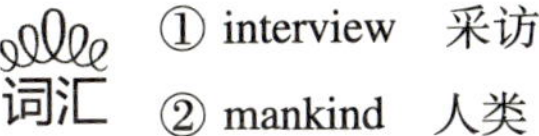
词汇

① interview 采访

② mankind 人类

采访上帝

“进来，”上帝对我说，“你想采访我？”

“是的，如果您有时间的话。”我说。

上帝笑了，笑容通过他的胡须绽开，说：“我的时间是永恒的，足以做任何事情。你心里有什么问题想问我？”

“对您来说，没有什么是新奇的。人类让您感到最惊奇的事情是什么呢？”

上帝回答道：“人类在孩童时期感到无聊，盼望着长大，长大后又向往着返回童年；他们牺牲自己的健康去赢得个人的财富，然后又花费自己的财富去重建自身的健康；他们焦虑地憧憬未来，忘记了眼前的生活，既不是为了现在也不是为了将来而活；他们活着，好像永远不会死去；他们逝去，似乎从未活过一样……”

上帝握着我的手，我们一阵沉默。过了好长一段时间，我说：“我可以再问您一个问题吗？”

上帝用微笑回答了我。

“作为天父，在新的一年里您会要求您的子民做什么？”

“去学习不要强迫别人爱自己，能做的是让自己被爱。

去了解信誉需要多年的努力去建立，但只需几秒钟就可以毁掉。

去懂得最有价值的不是他们生活中拥有的东西，而是他们生活里的人。

去懂得把自己和别人攀比是不好的，比上不足比下总是有余。

去明白富有的人不是他拥有得最多，而是他寄望最少。”

"Bricks" of Life

A young and successful executive[1] was traveling down a neighborhood street, going a bit too fast in his new Jaguar. He was watching for kids darting out from parked cars and slowed down when he thought he saw something.

As his car passed, one child appeared, and a brick smashed into the Jag's side door. He slammed on the brakes[2] and spun the Jag back to the spot from where the brick had been thrown.

He jumped out of the car, grabbed some kid and pushed him up against a parked car, shouting, "What was that all about and who are you? Just what the heck are you doing?" Building up a head of steam, he went on, "That's a new car and that brick you threw is gonna cost a lot of money. Why did you do it?"

"Please, mister, please, I'm sorry. I didn't know what else to do!" Pleaded the youngster.

"It's my brother," he said. "He rolled off the curb[3] and fell out of his wheelchair and I can't lift him up."

Sobbing, the boy asked the executive, "Would you please help me get him back into his wheelchair? He's hurt and he's too heavy for me."

Moved beyond words, the driver tried to swallow the rapidly[4] swelling lump in his throat. He lifted the young man back into the wheelchair and took out his handkerchief and wiped the scrapes and cuts, checking to see that everything was going to be okay.

"Thank you, sir. And God bless you," the grateful child said to him. The man then watched the little boy push his brother to the sidewalk toward their home.

It was a long walk back to his Jaguar … a long, slow walk. He never did repair the side door. He kept the dent[5] to remind him not to go through life so fast that someone has to throw a brick at you to get your attention.

Life whispers in your soul and speaks to your heart. Sometimes, when you don't have the time to listen, life throws a brick at your head.

It's your choice: Listen to the whispers of your soul or wait for the brick!

① executive 主管;行政官 ② brake 刹车;闸
③ curb 边石,侧石 ④ rapidly 迅速地
⑤ dent 凹痕

生活中的“砖头”

一个年少有为的总裁，以稍嫌快的车速，开着他的新捷豹经过住宅区的巷道。他必须小心孩子突然从停着的汽车背后跑出来，而当他觉得自己看到前方有什么时，就会减慢车速。

就在他的车经过时，一个小朋友出现了，丢了一块砖头，打到了他的车门。他很生气地踩了刹车，并后退到砖头丢出来的地方。

他跳出车外，抓住那个小孩，把他顶在一辆停着的车的门上说：“你这是怎么了？你是谁，你知道你刚刚做了什么吗？”接着又吼道：“这是辆新车，你知不知道要为刚才那一砖头赔多少钱？你到底为什么要这样做？”

小孩子求饶说：“先生，对不起。我不知道我还能怎么办。”

他接着说：“因为我哥哥撞到路边的石头，从轮椅上掉下来，我没办法把他抬回去。”

那男孩啜泣着问那个总裁说：“你可以帮我把他抬回轮椅上去吗？他受伤了，可他太重，我抱不动。”

这些话让这位年轻的总裁深受感动。努力平覆心中的感动之后，他抱起男孩受伤的哥哥，帮他坐回轮椅上，然后拿出手帕擦拭他的伤口，以确定他没有什么大碍。

那个小男孩感激地说：“谢谢你，先生，上帝保佑你。”然后总裁看着他推着他哥哥上了人行道，往回家的方向走去。

年轻总裁返回捷豹的路似乎很漫长，他没有修他汽车的侧门。他保留着车上的凹痕，为的是提醒自己：

生活的路上不要走得太匆忙，否则其他人需要向你扔砖头来引起你的注意。

生活与你的心灵喁喁细语，可有时，当你无暇去聆听的时候，它就会朝着你脑袋砸下一块砖头。

选择权在你：聆听心灵的话语或者等着挨砖头吧！

The Gift of Life

On the very first day, God created the cow. He said to the cow, "Today I have created you! As a cow, you must go to the field with the farmer all day long. You will work all day under the sun! I will give you a life span[①] of 60 years."

The cow objected, "What? This kind of a tough life you want me to live for 60 years? Let me have 30 years, and the 30 years I'll give back to you." So God agreed.

On the second day, God created the dog. God said to the dog, "What you are supposed to do is to sit all day by the door of your house. Any people that come in, you will have to bark[②] at them! I'll give you a life span of 30 years."

The dog objected, "What? All day long to sit by the door? No way! I'll give you back my other 10 years of life!" So God agreed.

On the third day, God created the monkey. He said to the monkey, "Monkeys have to entertain people. You've got to make them laugh and do monkey tricks. I'll give you 20 years' life span."

The monkey objected. "What? Make them laugh? Do monkey faces and tricks? Ten years will do, and the other 10 years I'll give you back." So God agreed.

On the fourth day, God created man and said to him, "Your job is to sleep, eat, and play. You will enjoy very much in your life. All you need to do is to enjoy and do nothing. This kind of life, I'll give you a 20-year life span."

The man objected. "What? Such a good life! Eat, play, sleep, do nothing? Enjoy the best and you expect me to live only for 20 years? No way, man! Why don't we make a deal? Since the cow gave you back 30 years, and the dog gave you back 10 years and the monkey gave you back 10 years, I will take them from you! That makes my life span 70 years, right?" So God agreed.

And that's why ...

In our first 20 years, we eat, sleep, play, enjoy the best and do nothing much. For the next 30 years, we work all day long, suffer and get to support the family. For the next 10 years, we entertain our grandchildren③ by making monkey faces and monkey tricks. And for the last 10 years, we stay at home, sit by the front door and bark at people!

词汇

① span　（某事物）自始至终的持续时间或期间

② bark　吠，叫

③ grandchildren　孙子孙女

生命的礼物

第一天，上帝创造了牛。上帝对牛说："今天，我创造了你。作为牛，你必须跟农夫下田，整天在日头下干活。我给你60年的生命。"

牛反对说："这样的苦日子，你要我忍上60年？我只要30年，另外30年你收回吧。"上帝答应了。

第二天，上帝创造了狗。上帝对狗说："你要整天坐在自家门口，有人进来就叫。我给你30年的生命。"

狗不乐意了，说："什么？整天坐在门口？绝对不行！我只要20年就够了，其余的10年还给你吧。"上帝答应了。

第三天，上帝创造了猴子。上帝对猴子说："你必须要猴把戏，逗人开心，让他们捧腹大笑。我给你20年的生命。"

猴子可不干，说："什么？逗人发笑？还要扮鬼脸，耍把戏？10 年就行了，剩下的 10 年你留着吧。”上帝答应了。

第四天，上帝创造了人。上帝对人说：“你只要吃喝玩乐，休息睡觉，舒舒服服地过日子就行了。别的什么都不用做，只管尽情享受。我给你 20 年的生命。”

人有意见了，说：“什么？吃喝玩乐，休息睡觉，安逸享受？这样的好日子，才让我活 20 年？啊呀，不行！你看这样好不好？牛还给你 30 年，狗还了 10 年，猴子也还了 10 年，就把它们还的时间全给我吧。这样，我就能活上 70 年了，对吧？”上帝答应了。

这下，你明白了吧……

最初的 20 年，我们吃喝玩乐，休息睡觉，安逸享受。随后的 30 年，我们整天工作个不停，辛辛苦苦地养家糊口。接下来的 10 年，我们扮鬼脸，耍把戏，逗孙子孙女们开心。最后的 10 年，我们终日待在家里，坐在门口，不住地对别人唠叨。

What Is More Important

An ironsmith[1] passed his time in singing from morning till night; it was wonderful to see, wonderful to hear him; he was more contented in soldering iron than was any of the seven sages. His neighbor, on the contrary, who was rolling in wealth, sung but little and slept less. He was a banker[2]; when by chance he fell into a doze at day-break, the ironsmith awoke him with his song. The banker complained sadly that Providence had not made sleep a saleable commodity, like edibles or drinkables. Having at length sent for the songster, he said to him, "How much a year do you earn, Master Greeley?"

"How much a year, sir?" said the merry ironsmith laughing, "I have reckoned[3] in that way, living as I do from one day to another; somehow I manage to reach the end of the year; each day brings its meal."

"Well then! How much a day do you earn, my friend?"

"Sometimes more, sometimes less; but the worst of it is, and, without that our earnings would be very tolerable[4], a number of days occur in the year on which we are forbidden to work; and the curate, moreover, is constantly adding some new saint to the list."

The banker, laughing at his simplicity, said, "In the future I shall place you above want. Take this hundreds of crowns, preserve them carefully, and make use of them in time of need."

The cobbler fancied he beheld all the wealth which the earth had produced in the past century for the use of mankind. Returning home, he buried his money and his happiness at the same time. No more singing; he lost his voice, the moment he acquired that which is the source of so much grief. Sleep quitted his dwelling; and cares, suspicions[5], and false alarms took its place. All day, his eyes wandered in the direction of his treasure; at night, if some stray dog made a noise, the dog was robbing him. At length the poor man ran to the house of his rich neighbor; "Give me back." said he, "sleep and my voice, and take your two hundreds of crowns."

词汇

① ironsmith 铁匠　② banker 银行家
③ reckon 认为;计算　④ tolerable 可容忍的
⑤ suspicion 怀疑

什么更重要

一个铁匠从早到晚在唱歌中度过。无论见到他本人或听见他的歌声都使人觉得很愉快。对于烙铁工作，他比当上了希腊七贤还要满足。与此相反，他的邻居是个银行家，拥有万贯家财，却很少唱歌，晚上也睡得不好。他偶尔在黎明时分迷迷糊糊刚入睡，铁匠的歌声便把他吵醒了。银行家郁郁寡欢地抱怨上帝没有把睡眠也制成一种像食品或饮料那样可以买卖的商品。后来，银行家就叫人把这位歌手请来，问道："格里利师傅，你一年赚多少钱?"

"先生，你问我一年赚多少钱吗?"快乐的铁匠笑道："我从来不算这笔账，我是一天一天地过日子，总而言之坚持到年底，每天挣足三餐。"

"啊，朋友，那么你一天赚多少钱呢?"

“有时多一点儿，有时少一点儿；不过最糟糕的是一年中总有些日子不准我们做买卖，牧师又常常在圣徒名单上添新名字，否则我们的收入也还算不错的。”

银行家被铁匠的直率逗笑了，他说：“我要你从今以后不愁没钱用。这200枚钱你拿去，小心放好，需要时拿来用吧。”

铁匠觉得自己好像看到了过去100年来大地为人类所需而制造出来的全部财富。他回到家中，埋藏好硬币，同时也埋葬了他的快乐。他不再唱歌了；从他得到这种痛苦的根源那一刻起，他的嗓子就哑了。睡眠与他分手；取而代之的却是担心、怀疑、虚惊。白天，他的目光尽朝埋藏硬币的方向望；夜间，如果有只迷途的狗弄出一点儿声响，他就以为是有人来抢他的钱。最后，这个可怜的铁匠跑到他那富有的邻居家里说：“把你的200枚钱拿回去，还我的睡眠和歌声来。”

Life Isn't a Competition

Dear Cecil,

You're only two years old, and at this point in your life you can't read, much less understand what I'm going to try to tell you in this letter. But I've been thinking a lot about the life that you have ahead of you, about my life so far as I reflect on what I've learned, and about my role as a mom in trying to prepare you for the trials that you will face in the coming years.

You are young, and life has yet to take its toll on you, to throw disappointments and heartaches and loneliness and struggles and pain into your path. You have not been worn down yet by long hours of valueless work, by the slings① and arrows② of everyday life.

There will be people in your life who won't be very nice.

They'll tease you because you're different, or for no good reason. They might try to bully you or hurt you.

There's not much you can do about these people except to learn to deal with them, and learn to choose friends who are kind to you, who actually care about you, who make you feel good about yourself. When you find friends like this, hold on to them, treasure[3] them, spend time with them, be kind to them, love them.

You will meet many people who will try to outdo you, in school, in college, at work. They'll try to have more luxurious cars, bigger houses, prettier clothes, more fashion gadgets. To them, life is a competition—they have to do better than their peers to be happy.

Here's a secret: Life isn't a competition. It's a journey. If you spend that journey always trying to impress others, to outdo others, you're wasting your journey. Instead, learn to enjoy the journey. Make it a journey of Happiness, of constant learning, of continual improvement, of love.

词汇

① sling 吊具;吊索;吊链

② arrow 箭

③ treasure 珍惜

生命不是一场竞赛

亲爱的塞西尔：

你现在仅仅 2 岁，此刻你还不识字，更不用说让你去理解我接下来想在这封信里对你所说的话了。但是我已经苦思冥想了好久，关于你即将面临的人生以及我的生活，我反思我所学会的；思考作为一个母亲的职责，力图让你为未来岁月中即将面临的困难做好充分准备。

你还很年轻，生命尚未开始摧残你，没有在你的人生道路上放置失望、伤心、孤独、挣扎和苦痛。你还没有被漫长的乏味工作，被日常生活的打击搞得筋疲力尽。

你的生活中一定会有并不友好的人。他们耻笑你是因为你不同，而再没有更好的理由。他们可能会欺负你或者伤害你。

对这种人你除了学会如何对付外无计可施。同时你也要学会择友，选择那些对你友善的，那些真正关心你的，那些令你自我感觉很好的人做朋友。当你寻找到像这样的朋友，就一定要坚守这份友谊，珍惜他们，花些时间和他们在一起，友善地对待他们并爱他们。

你会遇到一些人，他们总是试图超过你，无论是在中学、大学，还是在工作中。他们想要拥有更豪华的车，更宽敞的房子，更靓丽的衣物，更时尚的小玩意儿。对他们来说，生命就是一场竞赛——他们不得不比同辈做得更好来让自己感到快乐。

这里有一个秘诀：生命并不是一场竞赛，而是一段旅程。如果你在途中一直都试图给他人留下深刻印象，超过别人，那你就浪费了这段旅程。与之相反，学会享受它，让它成为快乐之旅，永恒的学习之旅，持久的进步之旅以及爱之旅。

There Are Two Kinds of Seas

There are two seas in Palestine. One is fresh, and fish are in it. Splashes of green adorn its banks. Trees spread their branches over it and stretch out their thirsty roots to sip of its healing waters.

The River Jordan makes this sea with sparking water from the hills. So it laughs in the sunshine. And men build their houses near it, and birds build their nests; and every kind of life is happier because it is there.

The River Jordan flows on south into another sea.

Here is no splash of fish, no fluttering leaf, no song of birds, no children's laughter. Travelers choose another route, unless on urgent and neither man nor beast nor fowl① will drink.

What makes this mighty difference between these neighbor

seas? Not the River Jordan. It instills the same good water into both. Not the soil in which they lie; not in the country round about.

This is the difference. The Sea of Galilee receives but does not keep the Jordan. For every drop that flows into it another drop flows out. The giving and receiving go on in equal measure.

The other sea is shrewder, hoarding[②] its income jealously. It will not be tempted into any generous impulse[③]. Every drop it gets, it keeps.

The Sea of Galilee gives and lives. This other sea gives nothing. It is named the Dead Sea.

There are two kinds of people in this world. There are two seas in Palestine.

① fowl 家禽

② hoard 贮藏

③ impulse 冲动

两片海，两种人

巴勒斯坦有两片海。一片是活水，鱼儿在水里游。大片的草地点缀着海岸。海边树木枝繁叶茂，饥渴的树根伸进海里，吮吸滋润的海水。

约旦河用源自山间的波光粼粼的溪水造就了这片海。于是海水在阳光下欢歌。人们在海边建房，鸟儿在海边筑巢，所有的生命都因为海的存在过着更加幸福的生活。

约旦河继续南流，流进另一片海。

这里没有游动的鱼儿，没有飘舞的树叶，没有鸟儿的鸣啭，没有孩子的欢笑。路人改道而行，除非事情紧急。不管是人还是走兽飞禽都不喝这里的水。

两片海相距不远，为什么差别竟如此之大？不能怪约旦河，因为注入到两片海里的约旦河水是一样的。也不能怪海水所在的土壤，或者海边的乡村。

区别在这儿：加利利海接纳约旦河水但并不守着河水一滴不放。约旦河每流一滴水，加利利海就流出一滴水。接受和付出以同样的速度在进行。

另一片海则更为精明，吝啬地把河水储存起来。无论你怎么利诱，它就是没有那种慷慨的冲动，滴水不放。

加利利海懂得付出，所以能活下来。另一片海丝毫不肯付出，人们称之为“死海”。

这个世界上有两种人，而巴勒斯坦有两片海。

Joy in the Journey

Two brothers decided to dig[1] a deep hole behind their house. As they were working, a couple of older boys stopped by to watch.

"What are you doing?" asked one of the visitors.

"We plan to dig a hole all the way through the earth!" One of the brothers volunteered excitedly.

The older boys began to laugh, telling the younger ones that digging a hole all the way through the earth was impossible.

After a long silence, one of the diggers picked up a jar full of spiders, worms and a wide assortment[2] of insects. He removed the lid and showed the wonderful contents to the scoffing[3] visitors.

Then he said quietly and confidently, "Even if we don't

dig all the way through the earth, look what we found along the way!"

Their goal was far too ambitious, but it did cause them to dig. And that is what a goal is for—to cause us to move on in the direction we have chosen; in other words, to set us to digging!

But not every goal will be fully achieved. Not every job will end successfully. Not every relationship will endure. Not every hope will come to pass. Not every love will last. Not every endeavor④ will be completed. Not every dream will be realized.

But when you fall short of your aim, perhaps you can say, "Yes, I did not succeed, but look at what I found along the way! Look at the wonderful things which have come into my life because I tried to do something!"

It is in the digging that life is lived. And I believe it is the joy in the journey, in the end, that truly matters.

词汇

① dig 挖,掘

② assortment 分类

③ scoff 嘲笑,嘲弄

④ endeavor 努力;尽力

旅途乐趣

兄弟两人决定在他们房子后面挖一个深洞。就在他们不停挖洞时，几个年龄大点的男孩在附近停下来观看。

“你们在做什么?”其中一个问道。

“我们计划挖一个洞，一直穿过地球到达另一端!”兄弟两个中的一个兴奋地抢先说道。

这些大男孩开始大笑，告诉这两个兄弟，挖洞穿过地球是不可能的。

长长的沉寂之后，其中一个挖掘者从洞里拿出一个装满蜘蛛、蠕虫和各种各样昆虫的罐子。他打开盖子把这些奇妙的东西展示给那些嘲讽者看。

然后，他平静而又自信地说：“即使我们挖不到地球另一端，但看看我们途中发现的东西!”

他们的目标是太过于雄心勃勃了，但确实激发他们去做了。而这，就是目标之所在——使我们朝着我们所选择的方向前进，换句话说，就是让我们去挖掘！

不是每一个目标都会完全实现，也不是每一样工作都能最终成功；不是每一种关系都能够持久，也不是每一丝希望都能够实现；不是每一次爱都能够天长地久，不是每一次努力都会硕果累累，也不是每一个梦想最终都能实现。

但当你没有达到预期目标时，也许你可以说："是的，我没有成功，但看看我们途中所发现的东西！看看这些因为我尽力去做而走进我生活的美妙东西！"

生命正是在挖掘的过程中才具有活力。而且我相信，到最后真正重要的还是过程中的乐趣。

Because You Are Special

A well-known speaker started off his seminar by holding up a $20 bill. In the room of 300, he asked, "Who would like this $20 bill?"

Hands started going up. He said, "I am going to give this $20 to one of you, but first, let me do this."

He proceeded to crumple[①] the 20-dollar note up. He then asked, "Who still wants it?" Still the hands were up in the air.

"Well," he replied, "What if I do this?" He dropped it on the ground and started to grind[②] it into the floor with his shoes.

He picked it up, now crumpled and dirty.

"Now, who still wants it?"

Still the hands went into the air.

"My friends, you have all learned a very valuable lesson.

No matter what I did to the money, you still wanted it because it did not decrease in value. It was still worth $20."

"Many times in our lives, we are dropped, crumpled, and ground into the dirt by the decisions we make and the circumstances that come our way. We feel as though we are worthless; but no matter what happened or what will happen, you will never lose your value."

"Dirty or clean, crumpled or finely creased, you are still priceless to those who love you. The worth of our lives comes, not in what we do or who we know, but by ... WHO WE ARE."

"You are special—don't ever forget it."

词汇

① crumple 弄皱,压皱;变皱

② grind 磨碎;磨成粉状;碾碎

因为你与众不同

一位著名演说家手里拿着一张 20 美元的纸币，开始了研讨会。在 300 人的屋子里，他问道：“谁想要这 20 美元纸币？”

开始有人举手。他说：“我会把这 20 美元纸币给你们中间的一位，但是，我要先这么做。”

他把这张纸币揉皱，然后问道：“还有人想要它吗？”那些手仍然举在空中。

“好的，”他说，“如果我这样做呢？”他把纸币扔到地上，开始用皮鞋使劲踩踏。

然后他拣起又脏又皱的纸币，问：“现在，还有人要它吗？”

空中仍举着很多手。

“朋友们，刚刚你们已经得出一个非常宝贵的经验。不管我怎么糟蹋这张纸币，你们仍然想要它，因为它的价值没有降低。它仍然是20美元。”

“在生活中，很多次我们被自己的决策和身边的环境所抛弃、蹂躏，甚至碾入尘土。我们感到自己一无是处。但是不管发生了什么，或者将要发生什么，你们永远也不会失去自己的价值。”

“无论你肮脏或者干净，皱巴巴的或者受尽折磨，对周围爱你的人来说你仍然是无价之宝。我们生活的价值不在于我们做了什么，或者我们认识谁，而在于我们是谁。”

“你是与众不同的，永远不要忘记这一点！”

Feather in the Wind

A certain kind woman one day said something hurt her best friend of many years. She regretted[①] immediately and would have done anything to have taken the words back. In an effort[②] to undo what she had done, she went to an older, wiser woman in the village, asked for help to win back the affection.

Listening to her, the older woman sensed[③] her distress[④] and knew she must help her. She also knew she could never alleviate[⑤] her pain, but she could learn a lesson at least. She said, "Tonight, take your best feather pillows[⑥] and put a single feather on each house in town before the sun rises."

The young woman hurried home to prepare for her chore, even though the feather pillows were very dear to her. All night long, she labored alone in the cold. At last the sky was getting light; she placed the last feather on the last house. Just as the sun rose, she returned to the older woman.

"Now", said the older woman, "go back and refill your pillows. Then everything will be as it was before."

"You know that's impossible! The wind blew away each feather as fast as I placed them on the house!" The young woman was surprised.

"That's true," said the older woman. "Never forget. Each of your words is like a feather in the wind. Once spoken, no amount of effort, regardless how heartfelt⑦ or sincere, can ever return them to your mouth. Choose your words well and guard them most of all in the presence of those you love."

词汇

① regret　为……感到遗憾;后悔;惋惜

② effort　努力

③ sense　侦测;感应

④ distress　苦恼

⑤ alleviate　减轻

⑥ pillow　枕头

⑦ heartfelt　衷心的

风中的羽毛

一个善良的女人有一次说了一些话，伤害了一个多年的好朋友。话一出口她就后悔了，她愿意做任何事来收回她说的话。为了收回她说的这些话，她来到了村里一位睿智的长者那里，寻求些建议来挽回这段友情。

听她说完后，这位长者感受到她的悲伤，决定帮助她。虽然年长的妇人知道不可能减少她的悲伤，但至少能让她吸取教训。长者说道："今晚，把你最好的羽绒枕头拿出来，天亮之前在镇子里每一户人家门口放上一根羽毛。"

年轻女人急忙赶回家，准备做这件事。虽然那些羽绒枕头对她来说非常珍贵。一整夜，她独自一个人在寒冷中辛苦劳动。最后，天快亮了，她在最后一幢房子前放上了最后一根羽毛。太阳一出来，她就来到年长妇人那里。

这位睿智的长者说道：“现在，再回去，用你放在房子前的羽毛把你的枕头装满。然后，一切就和以前一样了。”

年轻女人大吃一惊：“你知道那是不可能的！我在房子前每放一片羽毛，羽毛就立刻被风吹走了！”

年长妇女说道：“你说得对。不要忘了。你说的每一句话就像风中的羽毛一样。一旦说出口，不管你怎么努力，也不管你是多么真诚，再也不能收回了。因此你要谨慎地选择说的话，在你爱的人面前要更小心。”

Life Doesn't Have to Be Like That

A patient came to see me about the stress in her life. She described all the things she had to do—one was to make her bed—from the moment she woke up until she flew out the door for work. I suggested she experiment by not making her bed for two weeks. She was appalled[①], probably thinking I'd been raised by wolves in a forest. However, she went along with my idea.

Two weeks later she breezed into my office beaming[②]. She had left her bed unmade for the first time in 42 years—and nothing bad had happened. "And you know what?" she said. "I don't dry my dishes anymore, either."

This story illustrates an important principle about managing time: No one can do it all. Each of us has to make choices and accept trade-offs[③]. The problem is, many people choose in ways that put themselves and their health last. They take better care of their houses and cars than they do of themselves. They put everyone else's needs ahead of their own. That's fine if it's occasional. It would even be okay if there was a balance. But most people living that way are wearing themselves out, feeling out of control. Fortunately, life doesn't have to be like that.

Notice how it happens: Folks get busy and run short of time; they stop exercising or start skipping meals; next they steal time from their sleep. Soon they get too busy to see friends; they stop reading and playing ball, and six months go by without a long walk. That's not a great way to live.

So what is the solution? In a word, prioritize. Decide what you want in your life, and put that first. On a daily basis, that should include regular meals, adequate④ sleep and time with your family. Exercise, leisure, friendships and hobbies should also be regular aspects of life. The point is to do something for yourself every day. The choice is yours: whatever makes you feel good about yourself and your life. Take a nap. Take a walk. Take time to play the piano. Of course, you'll have to trade off some of things that are currently clogging⑤ your schedule to make room for your new priorities. Stop bringing your briefcase home from the office. Stop keeping your house as clean as your mother kept hers. Fill more of your time with want-to-dos instead of have-to-dos.

词汇

① appall　使胆寒，使惊骇

② beaming　喜气洋洋的，愉快的

③ trade-offs　取舍

④ adequate　充足的，足够的

⑤ clog　防碍，阻止；延迟

生活不必如此

有位病人来找我看病，她和我谈了她生活中的压力，描述了她不得不做的所有事情——其中之一就是铺床叠被——从起床那一刻起直到飞奔出家门去上班。我建议她试一试持续两周不要铺床叠被。她大吃一惊，很可能认为我是由狼在森林中养大的。但是，她还是同意了我的意见。

两周之后，她兴冲冲地来到我的办公室。这是她 42 年来第一次不叠被子——而且没有发生任何糟糕的事情。“你知道还发生了什么事吗?”她说，“我也不再揩干碗和碟子了。”

这个故事阐述了管理时间的一个重要原则：没有人能做完所有的事。我们每个人都得作选择，并接受有得必有失这一事实。问题是许多人选择将自己和他们的健康放在最次要的位置。他们对房子和车的关注甚于对他们自己的关注，满足别人的需要先于自己的需要。如偶尔为之还不错，若适度则更不错。但大多数这样做的人都活得很累，感到无法控制。所幸的是，生活不必这样。

注意这是怎么发生的：人们变得繁忙并且时间不够用；他们不再锻炼；开始饥一顿饱一顿；然后减少睡眠以得到更多的时间。很快他们变得太忙抽不出时间去看朋友；也不再读书、打球，甚至半年之内都没散过步。其实，生活本不该如此。

那么，该怎么解决呢？一句话，要确定优先级。生活中想要什么，就把它放在第一位。每天必做的事情包括固定的三餐饭、充足的睡眠、与家人共度的时光。锻炼、休闲、友谊和消遣也都应该成为生活常规的组成部分。关键问题是要为自己做些事情。由你来决定哪些事情能使你对自己的生活感觉良好。睡个午觉，去散散步，花点儿时间弹弹钢琴。当然，对最近那些占用时间太多的事必须权衡利弊做出调整，以便给新出现的需要优先做的事情腾出时间。不要再把公文包从办公室带回家。也不必像母亲那样把房子打扫得那么干净。用你的时间去做想要做而非不得不做的事情。

The Brother's Wish

A friend of mine named Abel received an automobile from his brother as a Christmas present. On Christmas Eve when Abel came out of his office, a street urchin[①] was walking around the shiny new car, admiring it.

"Is this your car, Mister?" he said.

Abel nodded, "My brother gave it to me for Christmas."

"I wish," the boy went on, "that I could be a brother like that."

Abel looked at the boy in astonishment[②], and then he added, "Would you like to take a ride in my car?"

"Oh yes, I'd love that."

After a short ride, the boy turned with his eyes aglow[③], said, "Sir, would you mind driving in front of my house?"

Abel smiled a little. He thought he knew what the lad

wanted. He wanted to show his neighbors. "Will you stop where those two steps are?" the boy asked. He ran up the steps. Then in a little while Abel heard him coming back, but he was not coming fast. He was carrying his little crippled[④] brother.

"There it is, Buddy. His brother gave it to him for Christmas and it didn't cost him a cent. And some day I'm gonna give you one just like it ... then you can see for yourself all the pretty things in the Christmas windows."

Abel got out and lifted the lad to the front seat of his car. The shined older brother climbed in beside him and the three of them began a memorable holiday ride. That Christmas Eve, Abel learned what Jesus meant when he said, "It is more blessed to give ..."

① urchin　顽童

② astonishment　吃惊

③ aglow　发亮的;通红的

④ crippled　跛的

哥哥的梦想

我有个朋友叫埃布尔，他的哥哥送给他一辆车作为圣诞礼物。圣诞节前夜，埃布尔下班走出办公室，看见一个淘气的小男孩绕着他那辆崭新的车欣赏着，不时地发出赞叹声。

“这是您的车吗，先生?”他问道。

埃布尔点了点头说：“这是我哥哥送给我的圣诞礼物。”

“我希望，”男孩继续说道，“我也成为那样的哥哥，可以送车给弟弟。”

埃布尔吃惊地看着男孩，问道：“你想坐我的车去兜兜风吗?”

“哦，当然想了，我太高兴了。”

他开了一会儿后，那孩子转过头来，用炽热的眼神望着埃布尔说：“先生，您能把车子开到我家门口吗?”

埃布尔微笑着，他以为自己知道小男孩想干什么，一定是想向邻居炫耀一番。“您把车子停在那两个台阶前好吗?”男孩问。男孩跑上台阶，不一会儿，埃布尔听到他回来的声音，但动作似乎较先前慢了好多。原来他领着他跛脚的弟弟来了。

“就是它，弟弟，是埃布尔的哥哥送给他的圣诞礼物，他没花一分钱哦。总有一天，我会送你这样一辆车，那样，到了圣诞节，你就可以自己去看商店橱窗里那些漂亮的饰品了。”

埃布尔下了车，把跛脚男孩抱到前座。哥哥兴奋的眼睛闪着奇异的光芒，他也爬上车子，坐到弟弟身边。就这样，三人开始了令人难忘的假日之旅。那个圣诞夜，埃布尔才真正领悟耶酥说过的道理：“施与比索取更幸福……”

Surrender to the Fact That Life Isn't Fair

A friend of mine, in response[①] to a conversation we were having about the injustices[②] of life, asked me such a question, "Who said life was going to be fair, or that it was even meant to be fair?" Her question was a good one. It reminded me of something I was taught as a youngster[③]: Life isn't fair. It is a bummer, but it's absolutely[④] true. One of the mistakes many of us make is that we feel sorry for ourselves, or for others, thinking that life should be fair, or that some day it will be. It's not and it won't.

One of the nice things to admit that surrendering to the fact that life isn't fair is that it keeps us from feeling sorry for ourselves by encouraging us to do the very best we can with what we have. We know it's not "life's job" to make everything perfect, it's our own challenge. Surrendering to this fact also keeps us from feeling sorry for others because we are reminded that everyone is dealt a different hand; everyone has unique strengths⑤ and problems in the process of growing up, facing the reality⑥ and making decisions; and everyone has those times that they feel victimized⑦ or unfairly treated.

The fact that life isn't fair doesn't mean we shouldn't do everything in our power to improve our own lives or the world as a whole. Just the opposite, it indicates that we should do it. When we don't recognize or admit that life isn't fair, we tend to feel pity for others and for ourselves. Pity, of course, is a self-defeating emotion that does nothing for anyone, expect to make everyone feel worse than they already do. The next time you find yourself thinking about the injustices of the world, try reminding yourself to this very basic fact. You may be surprised that it can nudge you out of self-pity and into helpful action.

词汇

① response 回答;响应

② injustice 不公平;非正义

③ youngster 孩子;少年;青年;年轻人

④ absolutely 完全地,绝对地

⑤ strength 力,力量;体力,力气;强度;浓度

⑥ reality 现实;实际

⑦ victimize 责怪或处罚某人不当(使之受冤或代人受过)

承认生活并不公平

和一位朋友就生活的不公平交谈时，她问我这样一个问题："谁说生活会是公平的，或生活应该是公平的?"这个问题问得好。它让我想起年轻时的一个教训：生活是不公平的。这让人不愉快，但确实是实情。我们许多人所犯的一个错误便是为自己或他人感到遗憾，认为生活应该是公平的，或者终有一天生活会是公平的。其实不然，生活现在不会是公平的，将来也不会。

承认生活并不公平这一事实的一个好处便是它激励我们去尽己所能，而不是自我感伤。我们知道让每件事情完美并不是"生活的使命"，而是我们自己对生活的挑战。承认这一事实也会让我们不再为他人遗憾，因为我们领悟到每个人都被分别给予一副不同的牌；每个人在成长、面对现实、作种种决定的过程中都有各自不同的能力和难题。每个人都会有感到成了牺牲品或遭到不公正对待的时候。

承认生活不公平这一事实并不意味着我们不尽自己所能去改善生活，去改造整个世界。恰恰相反，它正表明我们应该这样做。当我们没有意识到或不承认生活并不公平时，我们往往怜悯他人也怜悯自己，而怜悯自然是一种于任何人也无补的失败主义的情绪，它只能令人感觉比现在更糟。以后等你发现自己在思考世界上的种种不公正时，可要提醒自己这一基本的事实。你或许会惊奇地发现它会将你从自我怜悯中拉出来，采取一些具有积极意义的行动。

"Packaging" a Person

A person like a commodity[①], needs packaging. But going too far is absolutely undesirable[②]. A person should learn how to package a man.

A young person, especially a female, radiant[③] with beauty and full of life, has all the favor granted by God. Any attempt[④] to make up would be self-defeating. Youth, however, comes and goes in a moment of doze. Packaging for the middle-aged is primarily to conceal[⑤] the furrows[⑥] ploughed[⑦] by time. If you still enjoy life's exuberance enough to retain[⑧] self-confidence and pursue pioneering work, you are unique in your natural qualities and grace will remain. Elderly people are beautiful if their river of life has been, through plains, mountains and jungles[⑨], running its course as it should. You have really lived your life which now arrives at a complacent[⑩] stage of serenity[11] indifferent to fame or wealth. There is no need to resort to hair-dyeing—the snow-capped mountain is itself a beautiful scene of fairyland[12]. Let your looks change from young to old synchronizing[13] with the natural ageing process so as to keep in harmony with nature, for harmony itself is beauty, while the other way round will only end in unpleasantness. To be in the elder's company is like reading a thick book of deluxe edition that fascinates one so much as to be reluctant to part with.

As long as one finds one's own position, one knows how to package oneself, just as a commodity establishes its brand by the right packaging.

① commodity　商品,货物

② undesirable　不受大家欢迎的;讨厌的

③ radiant　放热的,发光的;辐射的

④ attempt　试图;尝试

⑤ conceal　隐藏;隐瞒;遮住

⑥ furrow　(脸上的)皱纹

⑦ plough　用犁耕田;耕

⑧ retain　保持;保留

⑨ jungle　(热带)丛林,密林

⑩ complacent　自满的,自鸣得意的

⑪ serenity　安详;宁静

⑫ fairyland　美妙神奇的地方;仙境

⑬ synchronize　把(钟表)拨至相同的时间,校准

人的包装

人如商品，要包装，但切忌过分包装。要学会给人包装。

年轻人，特别是年轻的女孩子，天生美丽，光彩照人，似乎上帝把最美好的东西都赋予了她。任何涂抹都是败笔。青春是打个盹就过去的东西。中年的包装主要是隐藏岁月磨损造成的皱褶，如果你依然享受生命的丰盈而保有自信，追逐事业的前沿，那么你便有独特的魅力，风采依旧。老人也是美丽的——如果他的生命之河按照既定的路程穿过了平原、高山和丛林。老人已经到达了一个宠辱不惊的知天命之年，真实地生活在人世间。所以，老年人不需要去染白发，老人的白发像高山的积雪，有种仙境之美。人该年轻时就年轻，该年老时就年老，与自然同步，这就是和谐。和谐就是美，反之就是丑。和老年人在一起就像读一本厚厚的精装书，魅力无穷，令人爱不释手。

人只要真正找到自己的位置，就知道该如何包装自己，正如商品通过恰当的包装而树立了自己的品牌一样。

The Rewards of Living a Solitary Life

The other day an acquaintance[①] of mine, a gregarious[②] and charming man, told me he had found himself unexpectedly alone in Paris for an hour or two if there is no date. He went to the mountain and spent the "empty" time looking at things in solitary bliss. For him it proved to be a shock nearly as great as falling in love to discover that he could enjoy himself so much alone.

Loneliness is most acutely felt with other people, for with others, even with a lover sometimes, we suffer from our differences of taste, temperament[③], mood. Human communication often demands that we soften the edge of perception, or withdraw at the very instant of personal truth for fear of hurting, or of being inappropriately present, which is to say naked, in a social situation. Alone we can afford to be wholly whatever we are, and to feel whatever we feel absolutely. What a luxury thing!

For me the most interesting thing about a solitary life, and mine has been that for the last twenty-five years, is that it becomes increasingly rewarding. When I can wake up and watch the sun rise over the ocean, as I do most days, and know that I have an entire day ahead, uninterrupted, in which to write a few pages, take a walk with my dog, lie down in the afternoon for a long think (Why does one think better in a horizontal position?), read and listen to music, I am flooded with happiness.

I feel lonely only when I am overtired, when I have worked too long without a break, when for the time being I feel empty and need filling up. And I am lonely sometimes when I come back home after a lecture trip, when I have seen a lot of people and talked a lot, and am full to the brim with experience that needs to be sorted out.

词汇

① acquaintance 熟人

② gregarious 社交的;群居的

③ temperament 气质;性情

独居所感

前几天，我一位善于社交、很有魅力的朋友告诉我，在巴黎没有约会的一两个小时感到莫名的孤单。他“没有活动的”时候就去山里，欣赏四周的美景，享受上天赐予的独居时光。他发现独处也能自得其乐时感到不胜惊讶，其惊讶程度之强烈并不啻于坠入爱河的感觉。

和其他人在一起时我们也能强烈地感受到孤独，因为和其他人甚至是爱人在一起时，我们有时也会因为双方的品味、秉性以及心情的差异而感到痛苦。人际交往常常需要我们收敛锋芒，坦白地说，当我们担心在社交场合道出实情会伤害他人或者不合时宜时，应该适时打住。当独处时，我们可以尽情地保留本色，尽情地回应自己的感受。这是多么奢侈的事情啊！

过去25年来，我一直过着独居生活。对我来说，这种生活最有趣的一点就是它变得越来越令人受益匪浅。我清晨醒来，看着旭日从海上升起，大多数日子我都是这样生活的，知道我接下来的这一整天都不会受到打扰，这段时间里我可以写几页文章，可以牵着小狗散步，可以在午后躺下沉思（为什么人在水平位置更善于思考?），可以阅读，可以听音乐，这时我的内心就会洋溢着幸福。

我只有在疲劳过度，长时间工作、半刻不曾消停，感到一时空虚、需要充实时，才感到孤单寂寞。有时当我演讲完回到家，当我见了很多人，说了很多话，需要整理自己丰富的经历的时候，我会感到孤单寂寞。

The Falling Kid

One afternoon, many years ago, I went to pick up my mother from work. I got there a little early so I parked the car by the curb, across the street from where she worked, and waited for her.

As I looked outside the car window to my right, there was a small park where I saw a little boy, around one and a half to two years old, running freely on the grass as his mother watched from a short distance. The boy had a big smile on his face as if he had just been set free① from some sort of prison. The boy would then fall to the grass, get up, and without hesitation② or without looking back at his mother, run as fast as he could, again, still with a smile on his face, as if nothing had happened.

I've always believed that in each of us is a little child with absolute[3] courage. A child that has the ability to run freely, or expresses himself fully and freely—without a care for anything external[4] and without a care for what people would say if he/she experiences a fall. I believe that the courageous[5] part of us, that courageous child within us all, will be always with us for as long as we live. We only need to allow it to emerge more fully. We only need to once again connect with that child within us and give that child permission to run freely.

词汇

① set free　使获得自由

② hesitation　犹豫，踌躇

③ absolute　绝对的，完全的

④ external　外部的，表面的

⑤ courageous　有胆量的，勇敢的

跌倒的小孩

多年前的一个下午，我驱车去接母亲下班。因为我到得稍微有点儿早，就把车子停靠在了母亲单位对面的路边上，等候母亲。

我透过车子的右窗，看见一个小小的公园，公园里有个小男孩，约莫一岁半到两岁的样子，在草地上自由地跑来跑去，他妈妈就在不远处看着他。小男孩笑得很开心，好像刚从牢笼里释放出来似的。他摔倒了，爬起来，毫不犹豫，也不回头看看妈妈，接着就跑啊跑，然后再摔倒，再爬起来，笑容始终挂在脸上，仿佛什么事都没发生似的。

从那以后，我就一直坚信，在我们每个人的内心都有一个勇敢无畏的孩子，一个能自由奔跑的孩子，或者无拘无束地展示自我的孩子——不在乎外界的事物，不在乎自己摔倒了人们会怎么说。我相信：只要我们活着，我们内心那个勇敢的部分，那个勇敢的孩子会永远与我们同在。我们只需要让他更彻底地释放出来，我们只需要再次与我们内心的那个孩子联接起来，允许他自由地奔跑。

图书在版编目(CIP)数据

像无人观望一样跳舞:英汉对照/浩瀚编. —厦门:厦门大学出版社,2011.11
(午后时光休闲阅读系列之智慧人生)
ISBN 978-7-5615-4041-1

Ⅰ.①像… Ⅱ.①浩… Ⅲ.①英语-汉语-对照读物②散文集-世界 Ⅳ.①H319.4:I

中国版本图书馆 CIP 数据核字(2011)第 202529 号

厦门大学出版社出版发行
(地址:厦门市软件园二期望海路 39 号 邮编:361008)
http://www.xmupress.com
xmup @ public.xm.fj.cn
厦门市明亮彩印有限公司印刷
2011 年 11 月第 1 版 2011 年 11 月第 1 次印刷
开本:889×1194 1/32 印张:2.75
字数:47 千字 印数:1～3 000 册
定价:14.00 元